GAMES
OF
SURVIVAL

TRADITIONAL INUIT GAMES
FOR ELEMENTARY STUDENTS

Published by Inhabit Media Inc.

Nunavut Office - P.O. Box 11125, Iqaluit, Nunavut X0A 1H0
Ontario Office - 146A Orchard View Blvd., Toronto, Ontario M4R 1C3

www.inhabitmedia.com

Written by Johnny Issaluk
Edited by Louise Flaherty, Neil Christopher, and Thomas Anguti Johnston
Photographs by Ed Maruyama

This book has been published with financial assistance from Canadian Heritage and the Qikiqtani Inuit Association.

We acknowledge the support of the Canada Council for the Arts for our publishing program.
Printed and bound in Canada.

Library and Archives Canada Cataloguing in Publication

Issaluk, Johnny, 1973-

Games of survival : traditional Inuit games for elementary students / written by Johnny Issaluk ; photos by Ed Maruyama.

ISBN 978-1-927095-21-8

1. Inuit--Games--Juvenile literature. 2. Inuit--Sports--Juvenile literature. I. Maruyama, Ed, 1978- II. Title.

E99.E7I77 2012   j306.4'830899712   C2012-904811-9

Canadian Heritage   Patrimoine canadien   Canadä

ᖃᖏᖅᑖᓂᒃ ᐃᓄᐃᑦ ᑲᑐᔨᖃᑎᒌᖏᑦ
Qikiqtani Inuit Association

Canada Council for the Arts   Conseil des Arts du Canada

ᓄᓇᕗᑦ Nunavut

GAMES OF SURVIVAL

TRADITIONAL INUIT GAMES FOR ELEMENTARY STUDENTS

Johnny Issaluk

INHABIT
MEDIA

TABLE OF CONTENTS

FOREWORD

I started playing Inuit games when I was thirteen, that young age when we become rebels and learn who we are. There were many days spent practicing and playing around doing kickstands. As I grew as a person, I grew as an athlete, and also I grew more connected to my history. Now, years later, I see that Inuit games taught me many things I use in life: strategy, endurance, strength, and above all, the importance of having fun.

There are three main categories of Inuit games: strength, endurance, and my favourite, agility. In the strength games you face an opponent, and you challenge that person to see who is stronger. In the endurance games, you see how much you can take compared to others. In the agility games, you are competing against yourself, demonstrating how much you have practiced. The games have come a long way, growing as Inuit grew, becoming more organized as Inuit organized. Games that were once played in iglus or on the ice now have an international presence. Friendly competitions between camps have become the Arctic Winter Games or the Northern Games. Now medals are handed out to the winners, and trophies to teams. And they are still a part of us. It is important that Inuit games are kept alive. They were meant to keep a hunter's mind clear and a hunter's body strong, and now they are used to bring Inuit together, from Russia to Greenland.

These competitions are where I feel closest to my ancestors. In competition, the agility games are the most challenging, requiring skill, confidence, and a lot of concentration, much like hunting for a family. Your opponents

become your team and the competition becomes more like a team event. The players begin to support each other, share pointers, and coach each other— all of a sudden everyone is on the same team. Everyone is working together.

Thomas Johnston

WHAT ARE INUIT GAMES?

The games came from hundreds of years ago, when Inuit lived in iglus and tents. They played the games so that they would be physically strong and mentally healthy enough to survive in the -50 degree weather in which they had to go hunting, catch caribou, and so on. And so that's why it's very important for me to share this knowledge with you and teach it to whoever wants to learn.

There are three basic types of games. **AGILITY GAMES** ensure that muscles are loose and joints are flexible, because sometimes Inuit had to chase wolves or caribou on rough, uneven terrain, so they had to be flexible. That way, they wouldn't get injured, and they could run for a long time. Agility games include the one foot high kick, the Alaskan high kick, and the one arm reach.

And then there's **STRENGTH GAMES**—the hunters didn't need to be the strongest, but they needed to be strong enough that if they caught a walrus or a whale off the floe edge with a harpoon, they'd be able to hold the animal as long as they had to. And so that's why they had strength games, such as the arm pull, the back push, and the hand pull.

This is also why **ENDURANCE GAMES**, like the knuckle hop, the running race, and the airplane, were crucial. Sometimes hunters would have to walk for a few days and catch the animal and come back carrying it, so they had no time to get tired. They always had to be healthy. That's why they were able to survive in the middle of nowhere, on the snowy tundra, with pana and harpoons and pitiksi. That's pretty incredible, and that's part of your lives, so that's why it's important for me to teach you.

Each of these games has a purpose—we'll learn these purposes at the same time as we learn how to play each game.

Johnny Issaluk

AGILITY GAMES

Agility games are the first of the three main parts of the Inuit games. These games loosen up your joints and your muscles, because traditionally, Inuit had to chase animals across rough terrain, like the tundra. If they were chasing caribou, for instance, they had to be flexible and agile so that they wouldn't get injured and they could run forever. It was crucial to their survival.

ONE FOOT HIGH KICK

To do the one foot high kick, you jump with both feet, bring one knee up, kick the target with the foot of that leg, and land on the same foot. This exercise loosens the muscles and keeps the joints flexible, since you use your whole body to jump up, your arms to pull yourself up, and then your knees and legs to kick fast and land.

1. Jump with both feet.

2. Bring one knee up and kick the target with your foot.

3. Land on the same foot that you kicked the target with.

TWO FOOT
HIGH KICK

The two foot high kick is the same as the one foot high kick, except that instead of kicking and landing with one foot, you kick and land with both feet at the same time.

1. Jump with both feet.

2. Kick with both feet at the same time.

3.   Land with both feet
      at the same time.

ALASKAN HIGH KICK

The Alaskan high kick requires that you balance on one hand, while holding one foot, and kick the target above you with your free foot, landing in the same position in which you started. To be in proper form, you have to remember to pull your chest up, and keep your movements as loose as possible.

1. Balance on one hand while holding one foot.

2. **Kick the target above you with the free foot.**

3. **Land in the same position that you started in.**

STRENGTH GAMES

Once your joints are loose and flexible from the agility games, you can do the strength games without getting injured. These strength games were traditionally played not for people to become the strongest, but for them to become strong enough to survive. For instance, historically, if someone was going to the floe edge to catch a whale, he would have a harpoon—back one hundred years ago they only had harpoons and rope, no guns—so he would have to catch the walrus or the whale and then he would have to hold it, until the animal would get tired. These days, I could just harpoon it and shoot it. But back in the day, they'd have to harpoon it and hold it, and if it was a walrus, they would have to get on the ice to hold it. That's why they had to be strong enough. Sometimes they would have to carry it home, and if the people at home in the village didn't get food they'd starve. Sometimes that happened.

And so that's why they had to be physically and mentally strong. Any sport you play in school, like basketball, soccer, volleyball, Inuit games—it's 80% mental. You have to think about how you're going to do it, and then envision yourself doing it. If you remember that, you'll be able to accomplish anything.

HAND PULL

The hand pull was traditionally used to strengthen the wrists and the grip, so that a hunter could hold a walrus in one place until the animal got tired. It also strengthened their arms and their backs, so they could lift the walrus if they were hunting alone.

This exercise requires two people. One person will be the anchor, keeping their body in place and providing resistance to their partner. The other person will be the puller, having to pull against the anchor, as if trying to pull that person out of water. It is important to remember to go slowly, and not to jerk, to avoid injuries.

This exercise requires one person to be the anchor, and one person to be the puller.

TRADITIONAL HAND PULL TOOL

Remember to use your back and legs!

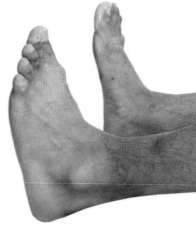

ARM PULL

Much like the hand pull, the arm pull has a purpose. When a hunter
was waiting for the walrus or whale to get tired, he would put the rope
around his arm and hold it there. So this game strengthens your arms,
your shoulders, and your back. In arm pull, you push with your leg, lock
your body, and start pulling back with your arms. For the strongest pull
possible, use every part of your body.

Push with your leg, lock your body, and start pulling back with your arms.

HEAD PULL

The head pull strengthens the shoulders, the neck, and the arms. This game requires two people. They put a band around their heads, and together they start pulling back.

ENDURANCE GAMES

Inuit played endurance games like knuckle hop, airplane, and running race, because traditionally they had to walk for days to get to where the caribou were, or where the seals were, or where the other animals were. And so they needed endurance to get to where the animals were, but not only that, sometimes they couldn't just ambush caribou, so they'd have to chase them. They had no time to be tired, and so that's why they had endurance games. Also, to get close to the seal, all they had were harpoons and hooks, and so they had to crawl for miles to get close to them before they could harpoon them. They needed the endurance to be able to catch seals this way. And once they caught them, they'd have to bring them back so their families could eat and not starve. There was no room for error.

KNUCKLE HOP

The knuckle hop is an imitation of the movement of seals. In this game, you keep your body straight, and your elbows as close to your body as possible. Then you hop straight up and down on your knuckles and toes, keeping your body as flat and rigid as you can.

1. **Keep your body straight, and your elbows as close to your body as possible.**

2. **Hop straight up and down on your knuckles and toes.**

Remember to keep your body as flat and rigid as you can!

AIRPLANE

To do the airplane, one person makes their body straight and flat, tucking their arms in on either side, while three people (one on either side and one behind the legs) lift him or her up in the air. You either measure time or distance, depending on whether the three people are just holding the person or are carrying the person.

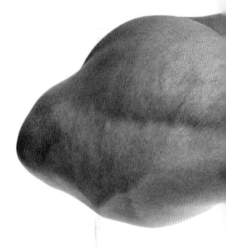

Arm position for the airplane

Remember to make your body straight and flat, and tuck your arms in on either side!

BACK PUSH

The back push is good for your arms and legs. Two people sit back to back with their feet flat on the floor and their knees in the air. Then they put their palms on either side of their legs and push hard, using both their legs and their hands, into the back of the other person.

1. Put your palms on either side of your legs.

2. Use both your legs and your hands to push hard into the back of the other person.

MUSKOX PUSH

Muskox push helps strengthen your shoulders, your legs, and your lungs. In this game, two people act like muskoxen with their shoulders locked together. Once both people are in position, they push hard against one another, building up endurance and also strength.

1. With your partner, lock your shoulders together like muskoxen.

2. Once both of you are in position, push hard against one another.

FINAL THOUGHTS

The games are as important as our language, our throat singing, and our drum dancing. They are vital because traditionally they were used not only for fun, not only for celebration, but for survival. And that is why a lot of us are here, because our ancestors created these ways to survive. They were inventive in every way possible, and they did it just to live day to day.

It's absolutely a privilege to be part of this book, to show the importance of our culture and tradition, and to have it recorded here for future generations. It's one of the biggest accomplishments of my life.

CONTRIBUTORS

Isimaili Qayaq

Johnassie Meeko

Johnny Issaluk

Kassidy Klinger

Monica Meeko

David Qayaq